# My Favourite Poem

# MY FAVOURITE POEM

An anthology of verse chosen by the famous in aid of The
Sharon Allen Leukaemia Trust

edited by
Mary Wilson

**CORGI BOOKS**

# MY FAVOURITE POEM

A CORGI BOOK 0 552 12713 2

First publication in Great Britain

PRINTING HISTORY
Corgi edition published 1985

Anthology Copyright © Sharon Allen Leukaemia Trust 1985

The copyright source for individual poems is given on pages 8 and 9

This book is set in 11/12 pt Garamond

Corgi Books are published by Transworld Publishers Ltd.,
Century House, 61–63 Uxbridge Road, Ealing,
London W5 5SA, in Australia by Transworld Publishers
(Aust.) Pty. Ltd., 26 Harley Crescent, Condell Park, NSW
2200, and in New Zealand by Transworld Publishers (N.Z.)
Ltd., Cnr. Moselle and Waipareira Avenues, Henderson,
Auckland.

Made and printed in Great Britain by
The Guernsey Press Co. Ltd., Guernsey, Channel Islands.

# ACKOWLEDGEMENTS

The Publishers are grateful to the copyright holders for granting them permission to reproduce the following poems in this anthology:

John Betjeman, 'Henley on Thames', from *Collected Poems*, John Murray (Publishers) Ltd.

C.P. Cavafy, 'Candles', from *The Complete Poems of Cavafy*, translated by Rae Dalven, reprinted by permission of The Hogarth Press and Harcourt Brace Jovanovich Inc.

Nurunnessa Choudhury, 'Sea and a Red Rose', reprinted by permission of The Basement Publishing Project.

Idris Davies, 'Land of my Mothers', from *Collected Poems of Idris Davies* reprinted by permission of Gomer Press.

C. Day Lewis, 'Walking Away', from *The Gate*, Jonathan Cape Ltd., reprinted by permission of the Executors of the Estate of C. Day Lewis.

Walter de la Mare, 'Silver', reprinted by permission of The Literary Trustees of Walter de la Mare and The Society of Authors.

T.S. Eliot, 'The Hippopotamus', from *Collected Poems 1909–1962*, Faber & Faber Ltd., reprinted by permission of Mrs Valerie Eliot.

Robert Frost, 'Never Again Would Birds' Song Be The Same' and 'Stopping By The Woods On A Snowy Evening', from *The Poetry of Robert Frost*, ed. Connery Latham, Jonathan Cape Ltd., reprinted by permission of the Estate of Robert Frost.

A.E. Housman, 'Tell me not here' and 'Bredon Hill', from *Collected Poems*, Jonathan Cape Ltd., reprinted by permission of The Society of Authors, representatives of the Estate of A.E. Housman.

Rudyard Kipling, 'If' and 'The Thousandth Man', from *The Definitive Edition of Rudyard Kipling's Verse*, reprinted by permission of the National Trust for Places of Historic Interest or Natural Beauty and Macmillan London Ltd.

Philip Larkin, 'The Trees', from *High Windows*, Faber & Faber Ltd., reprinted by permission of the author.

Louis MacNeice, 'The Sunlight on the Garden', from *Collected Poems*, Faber & Faber Ltd.

A.A. Milne, 'The More it Snows', from *The House at Pooh Corner*, Methuen Children's Books.

Kathleen Raine, 'Winds', from *Collected Poems*, George Allen & Unwin (Publishers) Ltd.

Victoria Sackville-West, 'The Greater Cats', reprinted by permission of Curtis Brown Ltd., on behalf of the Estate of Victoria Sackville-West.

Stevie Smith, 'Not Waving but Drowning', from *The Collected Poems of Stevie Smith*, Penguin Modern Classics, reprinted by permission of the Executor of the Estate of Stevie Smith.

Dylan Thomas, 'Fern Hill', from *Collected Poems*, J.M. Dent & Sons Ltd.

John Walsh, 'Good Friday', from *The Roundabout by the Sea*, O.U.P., reprinted by permission of Mrs A.M. Walsh.

Roger Woddis, 'Ethics for Everyman', reprinted by permission of *New Statesman*.

W.B. Yeats, 'The Song of Wandering Aengus', from *Collected Poems of W.B. Yeats*, reprinted by permission of Michael B. Yeats and Macmillan London Ltd.

Yevgeny Yevtushenko, 'When your face came rising above my crumpled life', reprinted by permission of Marion Boyars Publishers Ltd.

# PREFACE

I am very grateful to our distinguished contributors for so willingly sending their favourite poems — it is always a difficult task to choose one particular poem, and I was interested to find how many people chose one which was probably heard or learned in schooldays — a conventional poem, using rhyme and rhythm, to be recited to oneself and therefore easily remembered — and many of these poems contain a maxim.

Kipling's 'If' was popular — chosen by Prince Andrew, President Reagan and Jim Davidson; Mrs Thatcher and James Callaghan both chose Gray's 'Elegy in a Country Churchyard' also chosen by Philip Larkin, while the wry cynicism of 'Ozymandias' was chosen by Princess Michael and Tim Rice.

Ted Hughes, the Poet Laureate, paid tribute to 'Anon' in the poem 'Donal Og'.

Shakespeare is the favourite over all, although there were no duplications in the pieces chosen.

We have in this book a pleasing mixture of mainly well-known poems, interspersed with a few surprises, and representing a great range of diverse tastes. It is encouraging to know that so much poetry is still read and loved.

I hope you will all enjoy reading the book as much as I have enjoyed compiling it.


Mary Wilson

# FOREWORD

On behalf of the Trustees and Honorary Officers of the Sharon Allen Leukaemia Trust (SALT), I would like to express our gratitude and thanks to Mary Wilson for undertaking the arduous and painstaking task of editing this anthology of poetry. I doubt whether a single volume has ever contained such a distinguished number of people, in all walks of life, who have made their individual contribution to its success by choosing their favourite poem. To them, also, the Trustees and Honorary Officers of SALT express their thanks.

SALT, a new medical charity, was founded on 4 September 1984 to provide health care for sufferers from leukaemia and related disorders. We are the first charity to provide for the complete care of non-paying patients in the independent sector and in November 1984 we started holding bi-weekly clinics for SALT sponsored patients at the Churchill Clinic in London, where we funded our first bone marrow transplant. There are others in the pipeline. We are funding a research assistant who has developed, with the Chairman of our Medical Advisory Committee, a new immune treatment for leukaemia and we have set up a bone marrow transplant fund.

The Trust is named after Sharon Allen, a little girl from South London, who has leukaemia, a dreadful disease, which is the single biggest killer of children after road accidents. Our future plans are: to develop a sterile unit in London to minimise the risk of infection and increase the chances of recovery of patients undergoing chemotherapy or bone marrow transplants; to provide in-patient and out-patient accommodation and laboratory facilities; to build up our bone marrow transplant fund; and to develop other sterile units in National Health Service or independent hospitals elsewhere in the United Kingdom.

Unhappily, all the money needed for the treatment of leukaemia sufferers cannot be provided by the National Health Service. SALT exists to provide money from voluntary sources for people whose needs cannot be met from NHS funds and who could, in some cases, die if they had to wait for a bone marrow transplant, which they could not afford.

If those who buy this book, the royalties of which will go directly to SALT, would like to make an additional contribution to our work, they can do so by sending a donation to the Sharon Allen Leukaemia Trust, FREEPOST, London, SW1X OBR.


Humphry Berkeley
Director

# HRH PRINCE ANDREW
# PRESIDENT RONALD REAGAN
# JIM DAVIDSON

## IF——

IF YOU can keep your head when all about you
   Are losing theirs and blaming it on you,
If you can trust yourself when all men doubt you,
   But make allowance for their doubting too;
If you can wait and not be tired by waiting,
   Or being lied about, don't deal in lies,
Or being hated don't give way to hating,
   And yet don't look too good, nor talk too wise:

If you can dream—and not make dreams your master;
   If you can think—and not make thoughts your aim;
If you can meet with Triumph and Disaster
   And treat those two impostors just the same;
If you can bear to hear the truth you've spoken
   Twisted by knaves to make a trap for fools,
Or watch the things you gave your life to, broken,
   And stoop and build 'em up with worn-out tools:

If you can make one heap of all your winnings
    And risk it on one turn of pitch-and-toss,
And lose, and start again at your beginnings
    And never breathe a word about your loss;
If you can force your heart and nerve and sinew
    To serve your turn long after they are gone,
And so hold on when there is nothing in you
    Except the Will which says to them: 'Hold on!'

If you can talk with crowds and keep your virtue,
    Or walk with Kings—nor lose the common touch,
If neither foes nor loving friends can hurt you,
    If all men count with you, but none too much;
If you can fill the unforgiving minute
    With sixty seconds' worth of distance run,
Yours is the Earth and everything that's in it,
    And—which is more—you'll be a Man, my son!

*Rudyard Kipling*

*Dear Lady Wilson*

Thank you very much for writing to tell me about
the Sharon Allen Leukaemia Trust (SALT) and the
anthology you are producing as part of the fund raising
for a sterile unit at the Churchill Clinic.

It is wonderful to hear of the work being planned
by the Trust and I am happy to let you know that one
of my favourite poems is "Silver" by Walter de la Mare.

*With my best wishes*
*Alexandra*

## SILVER

Slowly, silently, now the moon
Walks the night in her silver shoon;
This way, and that, she peers, and sees
Silver fruit upon silver trees;
One by one the casements catch
Her beams beneath the silvery thatch;
Couched in his kennel, like a log,
With paws of silver sleeps the dog;
From their shadowy cote the white breasts peep
Of doves in a silver-feathered sleep;
A harvest mouse goes scampering by,
With silver claws, and silver eye;
And moveless fish in the water gleam,
By silver reeds in a silver stream.

*Walter de la Mare*

# BRIAN ALDISS

# THE WALLS OF EMERALD

1
Twelve turns of the rail on walls of emerald:
A sea-beast's horn repels the dust, a jade repels the cold.
Letters from Mount Lang-yùan have cranes for messengers,
On Lady's Couch a hen-phoenix perches in every tree.
The stars which sank to the bottom of the sea show up at
   the window:
The rain has passed where the River rises, far off you sit
   watching.
If the pearl of dawn should shine and never leave its place,
All life long we shall gaze in the crystal dish.


2
To glimpse her shadow, to hear her voice, is to love her.
On the pool of jade the lotus leaves spread out across the
   water.
Unless you meet Hsiao Shih with his flute, do not turn
   your head:
Do not look on Hung Ya, nor ever touch his shoulder.
The purple phoenix strikes a pose with the pendant of
   Ch'u in its beak:

The crimson scales dance wildly to the plucked strings on
  the river.
Prince O despairs of his night on the boat,
And sleeps alone by the lighted censer beneath the embroi-
  dered quilts.


3
On the Seventh Night she came at the time appointed.
The bamboo screens of the inner chamber have never since
  lifted.
On the jade wheel where the hare watches the dark begins
  to grow,
The coral in the iron net has still to put forth branches.
I have studied magic, can halt the retreat of day:
I have fetched phoenix papers and written down my love.
*The Tale of the Emperor Wu* is a plain witness:
Never doubt that the world of men can share this
  knowledge.

*Li Shang-Yin*

# KINGSLEY AMIS

## FROM LAST POEMS

TELL me not here, it needs not saying,
   What tune the enchantress plays
In aftermaths of soft September
   Or under blanching mays,
For she and I were long acquainted
   And I knew all her ways.


On russet floors, by waters idle,
   The pine lets fall its cone;
The cuckoo shouts all day at nothing
   In leafy dells alone;
And traveller's joy beguiles in autumn
   Hearts that have lost their own.


On acres of the seeded grasses
   The changing burnish heaves;
Or marshalled under moons of harvest
   Stand still all night the sheaves;
Or beeches strip in storms for winter
   And stain the wind with leaves.

Possess, as I possessed a season,
  The countries I resign,
Where over elmy plains the highway
  Would mount the hills and shine,
And full of shade the pillared forest
  Would murmur and be mine.


For nature, heartless, witless nature,
  Will neither care nor know
What stranger's feet may find the meadow
  And trespass there and go,
Nor ask amid the dews of morning
  If they are mine or no.

*A.E. Housman*

XXV - 1 - LXXXV

PIETRO ANNIGONI

Dear Lady Wilson,

My favourite poem is "L'Infinito" by
Giacomo Leopardi (1798 - 1837)

Wishing good success to your project

yours sincerely

Pietro Annigoni

17

# PIETRO ANNIGONI

## L'INFINITO

Sempre caro mi fu quest'ermo colle,
E questa siepe, che da tanta parte
Dell'ultimo orizzonte il guardo esclude.
Ma sedendo e mirando, interminati
Spazi di là da quella, e sovrumani
Silenzi, e profondissima quiete
Io nel pensier mi fingo; ove per poco
Il cor non si spaura. E come il vento
Odo stormir tra queste piante, io quello
Infinito silenzio a questa voce
Vo comparando: e mi sovvien l'eterno,
E le morte stagioni, e la presente
E viva, e il suon di lei. Così tra questa
Immensità s'annega il pensier mio:
E il naufragar m'è dolce in questo mare.

*Giacomo Leopardi*

# JEFFREY ARCHER

## THE THOUSANDTH MAN

ONE man in a thousand, Solomon says,
  Will stick more close than a brother.
And it's worth while seeking him half your days
  If you find him before the other.
Nine hundred and ninety-nine depend
  On what the world sees in you,
But the Thousandth Man will stand your friend
  With the whole round world agin you.


'Tis neither promise nor prayer nor show
  Will settle the finding for 'ee.
Nine hundred and ninety-nine of 'em go
  By your looks or your acts or your glory
But if he finds you and you find him,
  The rest of the world don't matter;
For the Thousandth Man will sink or swim
  With you in any water.

You can use his purse with no more shame
    Than he uses yours for his spendings;
And laugh and mention it just the same
    As though there had been no lendings.
Nine hundred and ninety-nine of 'em call
    For silver and gold in their dealings;
But the Thousandth Man he's worth 'em all,
    Because you can show him your feelings!


His wrong's your wrong, and his right's your right,
    In season or out of season.
Stand up and back it in all men's sight—
    With *that* for your only reason!
Nine hundred and ninety-nine can't bide
    The shame or mocking or laughter,
But the Thousandth Man will stand by your side
    To the gallows-foot—and after!

*Rudyard Kipling*

## A SILENT LOVE

The lowest trees have tops, the ant her gall,
The fly her spleen, the little spark his heat;
The slender hairs cast shadows, though but small,
And bees have stings, although they be not great;
   Seas have their source, and so have shallow springs:
   And love is love, in beggars and in kings.


Where waters smoothest run, there deepest are the fords;
The dial stirs, yet none perceives it move;
The firmest faith is found in fewest words;
The turtles do not sing, and yet they love;
   True hearts have ears and eyes, no tongues to speak:
   They hear and see, and sigh, and then they break.

*Sir Edward Dyer*

# VLADIMIR ASHKENAZY

## SONNET XXVII

Weary with toil, I haste me to my bed,
The dear repose for limbs with travel tired,
But then begins a journey in my head
To work my mind, when body's work's expired.
For then my thoughts (from far where I abide)
Intend a zealous pilgrimage to thee,
And keep my drooping eyelids open wide,
Looking on darkness which the blind do see:
Save that my soul's imaginary sight
Presents thy shadow to my sightless view,
Which like a jewel (hung in ghastly night)
Makes black night beauteous, and her old face new.
Lo thus by day my limbs, by night my mind
For thee, and for my self, no quiet find.

*William Shakespeare*

# ROWAN ATKINSON

See the happy moron
He doesn't give a damn
I wish I were a moron
My God, perhaps I am

*Anon*

# ALAN AYKBOURN

## MARCH TIME

The more it SNOWS tiddely-pom,
The more it GOES tiddely-pom
The more it GOES tiddely-pom
On Snowing
On Snowing.


And nobody KNOWS tiddely-pom,
How cold my TOES tiddely-pom
How cold my TOES tiddely-pom
Are Growing,
Are Growing.


Tra-la-la, tra-la-la,
Tra-la-la, tra-la-la.
Rum-tum-tiddle-um-tum.
Tiddle-iddle, tiddle-iddle,
Tiddle-iddle, tiddle-iddle,
Rum-tum-tum-tiddle-um.
   *(repeat)*

*A.A. Milne*

# PAM AYRES

## GOOD FRIDAY

How good to be once more in bed!
Smooth sheets, and coverlet of pink and grey!
To spread
Tired limbs and turn my thoughts upon
The things of the day!


All a long morning clear and fine
We worked, father and I, with garden hoe
And line,
To set the first seeds of the year,
Row upon row.


'No meals today!' And laughingly
Mother brought out a tray with buttered bun
And tea;
While Simpkin nosed the fence, and found
A place in the sun.


All afternoon we worked to trim
The lawns, while father joked and mother smiled
On him.

I moved between them, almost wanting
No other child.


Quietly at tea we sat; the clear
Flames crackled up from a fire of sticks and coal;
And near
My plate the yellow fluff-catkins stood
In their green bowl.


Now bed at last, with a warm drink . . .
Lying so curled, and hearing, as I lie,
The clink
Of cups as mother rinses them
And puts them by;


With sounds from out-of-doors half-heard
Voices; a starting car; the tiny cheep
Of a bird.
I do not think it will be long
Before I sleep.

*John Walsh*

# JILL BALCON

## WALKING AWAY

*For Sean*

It is eighteen years ago, almost to the day—
A sunny day with the leaves just turning,
The touch-lines new-ruled—since I watched you play
Your first game of football, then, like a satellite
Wrenched from its orbit, go drifting away


Behind a scatter of boys. I can see
You walking away from me towards the school
With the pathos of a half-fledged thing set free
Into a wilderness, the gait of one
Who finds no path where the path should be.


That hesitant figure, eddying away
Like a winged seed loosened from its parent stem,
Has something I never quite grasp to convey
About nature's give-and-take—the small, the scorching
Ordeals which fire one's irresolute clay.

I have had worse partings, but none that so
Gnaws at my mind still. Perhaps it is roughly
Saying what God alone could perfectly show—
How selfhood begins with a walking away,
And love is proved in the letting go.

*C. Day-Lewis*

# RONNIE BARKER

## WHAT LOVE IS

Love is the centre and circumference;
   The cause and aim of all things—'tis the key
To joy and sorrow, and the recompense
   For all the ills that have been or may be.


Love is as bitter as the dregs of sin,
   As sweet as clover-honey in its cell;
Love is the password whereby souls get in
   To heaven—the gate that leads, sometimes, to hell.


Love is the crown that glorifies; the curse
   That brands and burdens; it is life and death;
It is the great law of the universe;
   And nothing can exist without its breath.


Love is the impulse which directs the world,
   And all things know it and obey its power.
Man, in the maelstrom of his passions whirled;
   The bee that takes the pollen to the flower;

The earth, uplifting her bare, pulsing breast
    To fervent kisses of the amorous sun;—
Each but obeys creative Love's behest,
    Which everywhere instinctively is done.


Love is the only thing that pays for birth,
    Or makes death welcome. O dear God above
This beautiful but sad, perplexing earth,
    Pity the hearts that know—or know not—Love!

*Ella Wheeler Wilcox*

# HUMPHRY BERKELEY

## THE OLD VICARAGE, GRANTCHESTER

(*Café des Westens, Berlin, May* 1912)

Just now the lilac is in bloom,
All before my little room;
And in my flower-beds, I think,
Smile the carnation and the pink;
And down the borders, well I know,
The poppy and the pansy blow . . .
Oh! there the chestnuts, summer through,
Beside the river make for you
A tunnel of green gloom, and sleep
Deeply above; and green and deep
The stream mysterious glides beneath,
Green as a dream and deep as death.
—Oh, damn! I know it! and I know
How the May fields all golden show,
And when the day is young and sweet,
Gild gloriously the bare feet
That run to bathe . . .
                    *Du lieber Gott!*

Here am I, sweating, sick, and hot,
And there the shadowed waters fresh
Lean up to embrace the naked flesh.
*Temperamentvoll* German Jews
Drink beer around;—and *there* the dews
Are soft beneath a morn of gold.
Here tulips bloom as they are told;
Unkempt about those hedges blows
An English unofficial rose;
And there the unregulated sun
Slopes down to rest when day is done,
And wakes a vague unpunctual star,
A slippered Hesper; and there are
Meads towards Haslingfield and Coton
Where *das Betreten's* not *verboten*.


εἶθε γενοίμην . . . would I were
In Grantchester, in Grantchester!—
Some, it may be, can get in touch
With Nature there, or Earth, or such.
And clever modern men have seen
A Faun a-peeping through the green,

And felt the Classics were not dead,
To glimpse a Naiad's reedy head,
Or hear the Goat-foot piping low: . . .
But these are things I do not know.
I only know that you may lie
Day-long and watch the Cambridge sky,
And, flower-lulled in sleepy grass,
Hear the cool lapse of hours pass,
Until the centuries blend and blur
In Grantchester, in Grantchester. . . .
Still in the dawnlit waters cool
His ghostly Lordship swims his pool,
And tries the strokes, essays the tricks,
Long learnt on Hellespont, or Styx.
Dan Chaucer hears his river still
Chatter beneath a phantom mill.
Tennyson notes, with studious eye,
How Cambridge waters hurry by . . .
And in that garden, black and white,
Creep whispers through the grass all night;
And spectral dance, before the dawn,
A hundred Vicars down the lawn;
Curates, long dust, will come and go

On lissom, clerical, printless toe;
And oft between the boughs is seen
The sly shade of a Rural Dean . . .
Till, at a shiver in the skies,
Vanishing with Satanic cries,
The prim ecclesiastic rout
Leaves but a startled sleeper-out,
Grey heavens, the first bird's drowsy calls,
The falling house that never falls.

God! I will pack, and take a train,
And get me to England once again!
For England's the one land, I know,
Where men with Splendid Hearts may go;
And Cambridgeshire, of all England,
The shire for Men who Understand;
And of *that* district I prefer
The lovely hamlet Grantchester.
For Cambridge people rarely smile,
Being urban, squat, and packed with guile;
And Royston men in the far South
Are black and fierce and strange of mouth;

At Over they fling oaths at one,
And worse than oaths at Trumpington,

And Ditton girls are mean and dirty,
And there's none in Harston under thirty,
And folks in Shelford and those parts
Have twisted lips and twisted hearts,
And Barton men make Cockney rhymes,
And Coton's full of nameless crimes,
And things are done you'd not believe
At Madingley, on Christmas Eve.
Strong men have run for miles and miles,
When one from Cherry Hinton smiles;
Strong men have blanched, and shot their wives,
Rather than send them to St Ives;
Strong men have cried like babes, bydam,
To hear what happened at Babraham.
But Grantchester! ah, Grantchester!
There's peace and holy quiet there,
Great clouds along pacific skies,
And men and women with straight eyes,
Lithe children lovelier than a dream,

A bosky wood, a slumbrous stream,
And little kindly winds that creep
Round twilight corners, half asleep.
In Grantchester their skins are white;
They bathe by day, they bathe by night;
The women there do all they ought;
The men observe the Rules of Thought.
They love the Good; they worship Truth;
They laugh uproariously in youth;
(And when they get to feeling old,
They up and shoot themselves, I'm told) . . .


   Ah God! to see the branches stir
Across the moon at Grantchester!
To smell the thrilling-sweet and rotten
Unforgettable, unforgotten
River-smell, and hear the breeze
Sobbing in the little trees.
Say, do the elm-clumps greatly stand
Still guardians of that holy land?
The chestnuts shade, in reverend dream,
The yet unacademic stream?

Is dawn a secret shy and cold
Anadyomene, silver-gold?
And sunset still a golden sea
From Haslingfield to Madingley?
And after, ere the night is born,
Do hares come out about the corn?
Oh, is the water sweet and cool,
Gentle and brown, above the pool?
And laughs the immortal river still
Under the mill, under the mill?
Say, is there Beauty yet to find?
And Certainty? and Quiet kind?
Deep meadows yet, for to forget
The lies, and truths, and pain?. . . oh! yet
Stands the Church clock at ten to three?
And is there honey still for tea?

*Rupert Brooke*

# MELVYN BRAGG

## SHE DWELT AMONG THE UNTRODDEN WAYS

She dwelt among the untrodden ways
    Beside the springs of Dove,
A Maid whom there were none to praise
    And very few to love:


A violet by a mossy stone
    Half hidden from the eye!
—Fair as a star, when only one
    Is shining in the sky.


She lived unknown, and few could know
    When Lucy ceased to be;
But she is in her grave, and, oh,
    The difference to me!

*William Wordsworth*

# ELEANOR BRON

WHO hath herd of suche crueltye before?
  That when my plaint remembred her my woo
That caused it, she cruell more and more
  Wisshed eche stitche, as she did sit and soo,
Had prykt myn hert, for to encrese my sore;
  And, as I thinck, she thought it had ben so:
For as she thought this is his hert in dede,
She pricked herd and made her self to blede.

                              *Thomas Wyatt*

# LADY BUTLER OF SAFFRON WALDEN

## SONNET XCVIII

From you have I been absent in the spring,
When proud-pied April, dressed in all his trim,
Hath put a spirit of youth in everything,
That heavy Saturn laughed and leaped with him,
Yet nor the lays of birds, nor the sweet smell
Of different flowers in odor and in hue,
Could make me any summer's story tell,
Or from their proud lap pluck them where they grew.
Now did I wonder at the lily's white,
Nor praise the deep vermilion in the rose;
They were but sweet, but figures of delight,
Drawn after you, you pattern of all those.
   Yet seemed it winter still, and, you away,
   As with your shadow I with these did play.

*William Shakespeare*

# THE HIPPOPOTAMUS

*And when this epistle is read among you, cause that it be read also in the church of the Laodiceans.*

The broad-backed hippopotamus
Rests on his belly in the mud;
Although he seems so firm to us
He is merely flesh and blood.

Flesh and blood is weak and frail,
Susceptible to nervous shock;
While the True Church can never fail
For it is based upon a rock.

The hippo's feeble steps may err
In compassing material ends,
While the True Church need never stir
To gather in its dividends.

The 'potamus can never reach
The mango on the mango-tree;
But fruits of pomegranate and peach
Refresh the Church from over sea.

At mating time the hippo's voice
Betrays inflexions hoarse and odd,
But every week we hear rejoice
The Church, at being one with God.

The hippopotamus's day
Is passed in sleep; at night he hunts;
God works in a mysterious way—
The Church can sleep and feed at once.

I saw the 'potamus take wing
Ascending from the damp savannas,
And quiring angels round him sing
The praise of God, in loud hosannas.

Blood of the Lamb shall wash him clean
And him shall heavenly arms enfold,
Among the saints he shall be seen
Performing on a harp of gold.

He shall be washed as white as snow,
By all the martyr'd virgins kist,
While the True Church remains below
Wrapt in the old miasmal mist.

*T.S. Eliot*

# BARBARA CARTLAND

## TO YOU

Tiptoe away and close the Gates,
　The Gates of Dreams Come True;
Your chariot, Common Sense, awaits,
　To the world it must carry you.
Back again, perhaps you will say:
　'How silly was I to think
That Kindliness was the Golden Way,
　And Love ''the Missing Link''.'
Forget if you will, for a little while,
　Let the 'grown-up' part of you
Scoff with a supercilious smile
　At the thought of Dreams Come True.
But when the moon is very bright,
　And darkness hides the day,
You will see the sails of night
　Unfurl a familiar way. . . .
Blood red sails on an emerald sea,
　A silver moon above,
The good ship, 'ended Happily',
　Bound for the Land of Love.

*Happiness is in the mind. When you are tired, ill or miserable, try making a picture of beauty and tell yourself a story of love. If you do it frequently you will find yourself both happier and lovelier in body and soul.*

BARBARA CARTLAND

# LORD CHALFONT

## FERN HILL

Now as I was young and easy under the apple boughs
About the lilting house and happy as the grass was green,
    The night above the dingle starry,
        Time let me hail and climb
     Golden in the heydays of his eyes,
And honoured among wagons I was prince of the apple
        towns
And once below a time I lordly had the trees and leaves
     Trail with daisies and barley
    Down the rivers of the windfall light.


And as I was green and carefree, famous among the barns
About the happy yard and singing as the farm was home,
    In the sun that is young once only,
        Time let me play and be
     Golden in the mercy of his means,
And green and golden I was huntsman and herdsman, the
        calves
Sang to my horn, the foxes on the hills barked clear and
        cold,
     And the sabbath rang slowly
    In the pebbles of the holy streams.

All the sun long it was running, it was lovely, the hay
Fields high as the house, the tunes from the chimneys, it
was air
And playing, lovely and watery
And fire green as grass.
And nightly under the simple stars
As I rode to sleep the owls were bearing the farm away,
All the moon long I heard, blessed among stables, the
night-jars
Flying with the ricks, and the horses
Flashing into the dark.
And then to awake, and the farm, like a wanderer white
With the dew, come back, the cock on his shoulder: it was
all
Shining, it was Adam and maiden,
The sky gathered again
And the sun grew round that very day.
So it must have been after the birth of the simple light
In the first, spinning place, the spellbound horses walking
warm
Out of the whinnying green stable
On to the fields of praise.

And honoured among foxes and pheasants by the gay
        house
Under the new made clouds and happy as the heart was
        long,
    In the sun born over and over,
        I ran my heedless ways,
    My wishes raced through the house high hay
And nothing I cared, at my sky blue trades, that time
        allows
In all his tuneful turning so few and such morning songs
    Before the children green and golden
        Follow him out of grace,

Nothing I cared, in the lamb white days, that time would
         take me
Up to the swallow thronged loft by the shadow of my
         hand,
   In the moon that is always rising,
      Nor that riding to sleep
   I should hear him fly with the high fields
And wake to the farm forever fled from the childless land.
Oh as I was young and easy in the mercy of his means,
      Time held me green and dying
    Though I sang in my chains like the sea.

*Dylan Thomas*

# JOHN CLEESE

## ETHICS FOR EVERYMAN

Throwing a bomb is bad,
Dropping a bomb is good;
Terror, no need to add,
Depends on who's wearing the hood.


Kangaroo courts are wrong,
Specialist courts are right;
Discipline by the strong
Is fair if your collar is white.


Company output 'soars',
Wages, of course, 'explode';
Profits deserve applause,
Pay-claims, the criminal code.


Daily the Church declares
Betting-shops are a curse;
Gambling with stocks and shares
Enlarges the national purse.

Workers are absentees,
Businessmen relax,
Different as chalk and cheese;
    Social morality
    Has a duality—
One for each side of the tracks.

*Roger Woddis*

# JILLY COOPER

## THE ANCIENT MARINER

*An extract*

Beyond the shadow of the ship,
I watched the water snakes:
They moved in tracks of shining white,
And when they reared, the elfish light
Fell off in hoary flakes.

Within the shadow of the ship,
I watched their rich attire:
Blue, glossy green, and velvet black
They coiled and swam; and every track
Was a flash of golden fire.

O happy living things! no tongue
Their beauty might declare:
A spring of love gushed from my heart,
And I blessed them unaware:
Sure my kind saint took pity on me,
And I blessed them unaware:

The selfsame moment I could pray;
And from my neck so free
The Albatross fell off, and sank
Like lead into the sea.

*Samuel Taylor Coleridge*

# ROBIN DAY

## ODE TO THE WEST WIND

I

O wild West Wind, thou breath of Autumn's being,
Thou, from whose unseen presence the leaves dead
Are driven, like ghosts from an enchanter fleeing,

Yellow, and black, and pale, and hectic red,
Pestilence-stricken multitudes: O thou,
Who chariotest to their dark wintry bed

The wingèd seeds, where they lie cold and low,
Each like a corpse within its grave, until
Thine azure sister of the Spring shall blow

Her clarion o'er the dreaming earth, and fill
(Driving sweet buds like flocks to feed in air)
With living hues and odours plain and hill:

Wild Spirit, which art moving everywhere;
Destroyer and Preserver; hear, O hear!

## II

Thou on whose stream, 'mid the steep sky's commotion,
Loose clouds like Earth's decaying leaves are shed,
Shook from the tangled boughs of Heaven and Ocean,


Angels of rain and lightning: there are spread
On the blue surface of thine airy surge,
Like the bright hair uplifted from the head


Of some fierce Mænad, even from the dim verge
Of the horizon to the zenith's height,
The locks of the approaching storm. Thou dirge


Of the dying year, to which this closing night
Will be the dome of a vast sepulchre
Vaulted with all thy congregated might


Of vapours, from whose solid atmosphere
Black rain, and fire, and hail will burst: O hear!

## III

Thou who didst waken from his summer dreams
The blue Mediterranean, where he lay,
Lulled by the coil of his crystalline streams,


Beside a pumice isle in Baiæ's bay,
And saw in sleep old palaces and towers
Quivering within the wave's intenser day,


All overgrown with azure moss and flowers
So sweet, the sense faints picturing them! Thou
For whose path the Atlantic's level powers


Cleave themselves into chasms, while far below
The sea-blooms and the oozy woods which wear
The sapless foliage of the ocean, know


Thy voice, and suddenly grow grey with fear,
And tremble and despoil themselves: O hear!

## IV

If I were a dead leaf thou mightest bear;
If I were a swift cloud to fly with thee;
A wave to pant beneath thy power, and share

The impulse of thy strength, only less free
Than thou, O Uncontrollable! If even
I were as in my boyhood, and could be

The comrade of thy wanderings over Heaven,
As then, when to outstrip thy skiey speed
Scarce seemed a vision; I would ne'er have striven

As thus with thee in prayer in my sore need.
Oh! lift me as a wave, a leaf, a cloud!
I fall upon the thorns of life! I bleed!

A heavy weight of hours has chained and bowed
One too like thee: tameless, and swift, and proud.

## V

Make me thy lyre, even as the forest is:
What if my leaves are falling like its own!
The tumult of thy mighty harmonies

Will take from both a deep, autumnal tone,
Sweet though in sadness. Be thou, Spirit fierce,
My spirit! Be thou me, impetuous one!

Drive my dead thoughts over the universe
Like withered leaves to quicken a new birth!
And, by the incantation of this verse,

Scatter, as from an unextinguished hearth
Ashes and sparks, my words among mankind!
Be through my lips to unawakened Earth

The trumpet of a prophecy! O Wind,
If Winter comes, can Spring be far behind?

*Percy Bysshe Shelley*

# GAVIN EWART

## A NOCTURNAL UPON ST LUCY'S DAY, BEING THE SHORTEST DAY

'Tis the year's midnight, and it is the day's,
Lucy's, who scarce seven hours herself unmasks;
   The Sun is spent, and now his flasks
   Send forth light squibs, no constant rays;
     The world's whole sap is sunk:
The general balm th' hydroptic earth hath drunk,
Whither, as to the bed's-feet, life is shrunk,
Dead and interr'd; yet all these seem to laugh,
Compar'd with me, who am their Epitaph.


Study me then, you who shall lovers be
At the next world, that is, at the next Spring:
   For I am every dead thing,
   In whom love wrought new alchemy.
     For his art did express
A quintessence even from nothingness,
From dull privations, and lean emptiness:
He ruin'd me, and I am re-begot
Of absence, darkness, death; things which are not.

All others, from all things, draw all that's good,
Life, soul, form, spirit, whence they being have;
   I, by love's limbec, am the grave
  Of all, that's nothing. Oft a flood
     Have we two wept, and so
Drown'd the whole world, us two; oft did we grow
To be two Chaoses, when we did show
Care to aught else; and often absences
Withdrew our souls, and made us carcases.


But I am by her death (which word wrongs her)
Of the first nothing, the Elixir grown;
   Were I a man, that I were one,
  I needs must know; I should prefer,
     If I were any beast,
Some ends, some means; yea plants, yea stones detest,
And love; all, all some properties invest;
If I an ordinary nothing were,
As shadow, a light, and body must be here.

But I am None; nor will my Sun renew.
You lovers, for whose sake, the lesser Sun
   At this time to the Goat is run
   To fetch new lust, and give it you,
     Enjoy your summer all;
Since she enjoys her long night's festival,
Let me prepare towards her, and let me call
This hour her Vigil, and her Eve, since this
Both the year's, and the day's deep midnight is.

*John Donne*

# LADY FALKENDER

## ODE ON INTIMATIONS OF IMMORTALITY FROM RECOLLECTIONS OF EARLY CHILDHOOD

*An extract*

Our birth is but a sleep and a forgetting:
The Soul that rises with us, our life's Star,
    Hath had elsewhere its setting,
       And cometh from afar:
     Not in entire forgetfulness,
     And not in utter nakedness,
But trailing clouds of glory do we come
    From God, who is our home:
Heaven lies about us in our infancy!
Shades of the prison-house begin to close
    Upon the growing Boy,
But He beholds the light, and whence it flows,
    He sees it in his joy;
The Youth, who daily farther from the east
    Must travel, still is Nature's Priest,

And by the vision splendid
　Is on his way attended;
At length the Man perceives it die away,
And fade into the light of common day.

*William Wordsworth*

# MICHAEL FOOT

## DARKNESS

I HAD a dream, which was not all a dream.
The bright sun was extinguish'd, and the stars
Did wander darkling in the eternal space,
Rayless, and pathless, and the icy earth
Swung blind and blackening in the moonless air;
Morn came and went—and came, and brought no day,
And men forgot their passions in the dread
Of this their desolation; and all hearts
Were chill'd into a selfish prayer for light:
And they did live by watchfires—and the thrones,
The palaces of crowned kings—the huts,
The habitations of all things which dwell,
Were burnt for beacons; cities were consumed,
And men were gather'd round their blazing homes
To look once more into each other's face;
Happy were those who dwelt within the eye
Of the volcanos, and their mountain-torch:
A fearful hope was all the world contain'd;
Forests were set on fire—but hour by hour
They fell and faded—and the crackling trunks
Extinguish'd with a crash—and all was black.
The brows of men by the despairing light
Wore an unearthly aspect, as by fits

The flashes fell upon them; some lay down
And hid their eyes and wept; and some did rest
Their chins upon their clenched hands, and smiled;
And others hurried to and fro, and fed
Their funeral piles with fuel, and look'd up
With mad disquietude on the dull sky,
The pall of a past world; and then again
With curses cast them down upon the dust,
And gnash'd their teeth and howl'd: the wild birds shriek'd
And, terrified, did flutter on the ground,
And flap their useless wings; the wildest brutes
Came tame and tremulous; and vipers crawl'd
And twined themselves among the multitude,
Hissing, but stingless—they were slain for food.
And War, which for a moment was no more,
Did glut himself again:—a meal was bought
With blood, and each sate sullenly apart
Gorging himself in gloom: no love was left;
All earth was but one thought—and that was death
Immediate and inglorious; and the pang
Of famine fed upon all entrails—men
Died, and their bones were tombless as their flesh;
The meagre by the meagre were devour'd,

Even dogs assail'd their masters, all save one,
And he was faithful to a corse, and kept
The birds and beasts and famish'd men at bay,
Till hunger clung them, or the dropping dead
Lured their lank jaws; himself sought out no food,
But with a piteous and perpetual mean,
And a quick desolate cry, licking the hand
Which answer'd not with a caress—he died.
The crowd was famish'd by degrees; but two
Of an enormous city did survive,
And they were enemies: they met beside
The dying embers of an altar-place
Where had been heap'd a mass of holy things
For an unholy usage; they raked up,
And shivering scraped with their cold skeleton hands
The feeble ashes, and their feeble breath
Blew for a little life, and made a flame
Which was a mockery; then they lifted up
Their eyes as it grew lighter, and beheld
Each other's aspects—saw, and shriek'd, and died—
Even of their mutual hideousness they died,
Unknowing who he was upon whose brow
Famine had written Fiend. The world was void,

The populous and the powerful was a lump,
Seasonless, herbless, treeless, manless, lifeless,
A lump of death—a chaos of hard clay.
The rivers, lakes, and ocean all stood still,
And nothing stirr'd within their silent depths;
Ships sailorless lay rotting on the sea,
And their masts fell down piecemeal: as they dropp'd
They slept on the abyss without a surge—
The waves were dead; the tides were in their grave,
The moon, their mistress, had expired before;
The winds were wither'd in the stagnant air,
And the clouds perish'd; Darkness had no need
Of aid from them—She was the Universe.

                            Diodati, *July* 1816.


*Lord Byron*

# FREDERICK FORSYTH

## THE BURIAL OF SIR JOHN MOORE
## AT CORUNNA

Not a drum was heard, not a funeral note,
  As his corpse to the rampart we hurried;
Not a soldier discharged his farewell shot
  O'er the grave where our hero we buried..

We buried him darkly at dead of night,
  The sods with our bayonets turning;
By the struggling moonbeam's misty light
  And the lantern dimly burning.

No useless coffin enclosed his breast,
    Not in sheet nor in shroud we wound him;
But he lay like a warrior taking his rest
    With his martial cloak around him.


Few and short were the prayers we said,
    And we spoke not a word of sorrow;
But we steadfastly gazed on the face that was dead,
    And we bitterly thought of the morrow.


We thought, as we hollow'd his narrow bed
    And smoothed down his lonely pillow,
That the foe and the stranger would tread o'er his head,
    And we far away on the billow!


Lightly they'll talk of the spirit that's gone
    And o'er his cold ashes upbraid him,—
But little he'll reck, if they let him sleep on
    In the grave where a Briton has laid him.

But half of our heavy task was done
   When the clock struck the hour for retiring:
And we heard the distant and random gun
   That the foe was sullenly firing.

Slowly and sadly we laid him down,
   From the field of his fame fresh and gory;
We carved not a line, and we raised not a stone—
   But we left him alone with his glory.

*Charles Wolfe*

# ANTONIA FRASER

## TRUE LOVE

LET me not to the marriage of true minds
Admit impediments. Love is not love
Which alters when it alteration finds,
Or bends with the remover to remove:—

O no! it is an ever-fixéd mark
That looks on tempests, and is never shaken;
It is the star to every wandering bark,
Whose worth's unknown, although his height be taken.

Love's not Time's fool, though rosy lips and cheeks
Within his bending sickle's compass come;
Love alters not with his brief hours and weeks,
But bears it out ev'n to the edge of doom:—

If this be error, and upon me proved,
I never writ, nor no man ever loved.

*William Shakespeare*

# ROY FULLER

## THE SEVEN TIMES

THE dark was thick. A boy he seemed at that time
   Who trotted by me with uncertain air;
'I'll tell my tale,' he murmured, 'for I fancy
     A friend goes there? . . .'


Then thus he told. 'I reached—'twas for the first time—
   A dwelling. Life was clogged in me with care;
I thought not I should meet an eyesome maiden,
     But found one there.


'I entered on the precincts for the second time—
   'Twas an adventure fit and fresh and fair—
I slackened in my footsteps at the porchway,
     And found her there.


'I rose and travelled thither for the third time,
   The hope-hues growing gayer and yet gayer
As I hastened round the boscage of the outskirts,
     And found her there.

'I journeyed to the place again the fourth time
    (The best and rarest visit of the rare,
As it seemed to me, engrossed about these goings),
        And found her there.


'When I bent me to my pilgrimage the fifth time
    (Soft-thinking as I journeyed I would dare
A certain word at token of good auspice),
        I found her there.


'That landscape did I traverse for the sixth time,
    And dreamed on what we purposed to prepare;
I reached a tryst before my journey's end came,
        And found her there.


'I went again—long after—aye, the seventh time;
    The look of things was sinister and bare
As I caught no customed signal, heard no voice call,
        Nor found her there.

'And now I gad the globe—day, night, and any time,
   To light upon her hiding unaware,
And, maybe, I shall nigh me to some nymph-niche,
      And find her there!'


'But how,' said I, 'has your so little lifetime
   Given roomage for such loving, loss, despair?
A boy so young!' Forthwith I turned my lantern
      Upon him there.


His head was white. His small form, fine aforetime,
   Was shrunken with old age and battering wear,
An eighty-years long plodder saw I pacing
      Beside me there.

*Thomas Hardy*

# TED HUGHES
## *(Poet Laureate)*

## DONAL ÓG

It is late last night the dog was speaking of you;
the snipe was speaking of you in her deep marsh.
It is you are the lonely bird through the woods;
and that you may be without a mate until you find me.

You promised me, and you said a lie to me,
that you would be before me where the sheep are flocked;
I gave a whistle and three hundred cries to you,
and I found nothing there but a bleating lamb.

You promised me a thing that was hard for you,
a ship of gold under a silver mast;
twelve towns with a market in all of them,
and a fine white court by the side of the sea.

You promised me a thing that is not possible,
that you would give me gloves of the skin of a fish;
that you would give me shoes of the skin of a bird;
and a suit of the dearest silk in Ireland.

When I go by myself to the Well of Loneliness,
I sit down and I go through my trouble;
when I see the world and do not see my boy,
he that has an amber shade in his hair.

It was on that Sunday I gave my love to you;
the Sunday that is last before Easter Sunday.
And myself on my knees reading the Passion;
and my two eyes giving love to you for ever.

My mother said to me not to be talking with you today,
or tomorrow, or on the Sunday;
it was a bad time she took for telling me that;
it was shutting the door after the house was robbed.

My heart is as black as the blackness of the sloe,
or as the black coal that is on the smith's forge;
or as the sole of a shoe left in white halls;
it was you put that darkness over my life.

You have taken the east from me; you have taken the west
   from me;
you have taken what is before me and what is behind me;
you have taken the moon, you have taken the sun from me;
and my fear is great that you have taken God from me!

*Anon*

From the Irish (trans. Lady Augusta Gregory)

# JOHN GIELGUD

## BREDON HILL

IN summertime on Bredon
  The bells they sound so clear;
Round both the shires they ring them
  In steeples far and near,
  A happy noise to hear.


Here of a Sunday morning
  My love and I would lie,
And see the coloured counties,
  And hear the larks so high
  About us in the sky.


The bells would ring to call her
  In valleys miles away:
'Come all to church, good people;
  Good people, come and pray.'
  But here my love would stay.

And I would turn and answer
   Among the springing thyme,
'Oh, peal upon our wedding,
   And we will hear the chime,
   And come to church in time.'

But when the snows at Christmas
   On Bredon top were strown,
My love rose up so early
   And stole out unbeknown
   And went to church alone.

They tolled the one bell only,
   Groom there was none to see,
The mourners followed after,
   And so to church went she,
   And would not wait for me.

The bells they sound on Bredon,
 And still the steeples hum.
'Come all to church, good people,'—
 Oh, noisy bells, be dumb;
 I hear you, I will come.

*A.E. Housman*
*The Shropshire Lad*

## LORD GOWRIE

# NEVER AGAIN WOULD BIRD'S SONG BE THE SAME

He would declare and could himself believe
That the birds there in all the garden round
From having heard the daylong voice of Eve
Had added to their own an oversound,
Her tone of meaning but without the words.
Admittedly an eloquence so soft
Could only have had an influence on birds
When call or laughter carried it aloft.
Be that as may be, she was in their song.
Moreover her voice upon their voices crossed
Had now persisted in the woods so long
That probably it never would be lost.
Never again would birds' song be the same.
And to do that to birds was why she came.

*Robert Frost*

# ELSPET GRAY

## WINDS

I have heard all day the voices
On the hills the loud winds
Utter from no place, clamour
Of bodies of air, speeding, whirling
Stream of invisible
Elements crying that are not,
Were, may be, living
The fields of the grass, lifting
Leaves of the forests, are not, have been, would be
Breath of all sentient beings, long lamentation
For living and loving and knowing, states of being
The wandering winds cannot
Discover for ever for all their seeking and wailing.

*Kathleen Raine*

# GRAHAM GREENE

## ANDREA DEL SARTO (CALLED 'THE FAULTLESS PAINTER')

*An extract*

Behold Madonna!—I am bold to say.
I can do with my pencil what I know,
What I see, what at bottom of my heart
I wish for, if I ever wish so deep—
Do easily, too—when I say, perfectly,
I do not boast, perhaps: yourself are judge,
Who listened to the Legate's talk last week,
And just as much they used to say in France.
At any rate 't is easy, all of it!
No sketches first, no studies, that's long past:
I do what many dream of, all their lives,
—Dream? strive to do, and agonize to do,
And fail in doing. I could count twenty such
On twice your fingers, and not leave this town,
Who strive—you don't know how the others strive
To paint a little thing like that you smeared
Carelessly passing with your robes afloat,—
Yet do much less, so much less, Someone says,
(I know his name, no matter)—so much less!
Well, less is more, Lucrezia: I am judged.

There burns a truer light of God in them.
In their vexed beating stuffed and stopped-up brain,
Heart, or whate'er else, than goes on to prompt
This low-pulsed forthright craftsman's hand of mine.
Their works drop groundward, but themselves, I know,
Reach many a time a heaven that's shut to me,
Enter and take their place there sure enough,
Though they come back and cannot tell the world.
My works are nearer heaven, but I sit here.
The sudden blood of these men! at a word—
Praise them, it boils, or blame them, it boils too.
I, painting from myself and to myself,
Know what I do, am unmoved by men's blame
Or their praise either. Somebody remarks
Morello's outline there is wrongly traced,
His hue mistaken; what of that? or else,
Rightly traced and well ordered; what of that?
Speak as they please, what does the mountain care?
Ah, but a man's reach should exceed his grasp,
Or what's a heaven for?

*Robert Browning*

# ALEC GUINNESS

## THE NIGHT

Through that pure Virgin-shrine,
That sacred veil drawn o'er thy glorious noon
That men might look and live as Glow-worms shine,
    And face the Moon:
  Wise Nicodemus saw such light
  As made him know his God by night.


Most blest believer he!
Who in that land of darkness and blind eyes
Thy long expected healing wings could see,
    When thou didst rise,
  And what can never more be done,
  Did at mid-night speak with the Sun!


O who will tell me, where
He found thee at that dead and silent hour!
What hallow'd solitary ground did bear
    So rare a flower,
  Within whose sacred leafs did lie
  The fulness of the Deity.

No mercy-seat of gold,
No dead and dusty Cherub, nor carv'd stone,
But his own living works did my Lord hold
    And lodge alone;
  Where trees and herbs did watch and peep
  And wonder, while the Jews did sleep.


    Dear night! this world's defeat;
The stop to busy fools; care's check and curb;
The day of spirits; my soul's calm retreat
    Which none disturb!
Christ's progress, and his prayer time;
The hours to which high Heaven doth chime.


    God's silent, searching flight:
When my Lord's head is fill'd with dew, and all
His locks are wet with the clear drops of night;
    His still, soft call;
His knocking time; The soul's dumb watch,
  When spirits their fair kindred catch.

Were all my loud, evil days
Calm and unhaunted as is thy dark Tent,
Whose peace but by some Angel's wing or voice
        Is seldom rent;
    Then I in Heaven all the long year
    Would keep, and never wander here.


        But living where the Sun
Doth all things wake, and where all mix and tire
Themselves and others, I consent and run
        To every mire,
    And by this world's ill-guiding light,
    Err more than I can do by night.


        There is in God (some say)
A deep, but dazzling darkness; As men here
Say it is late and dusky, because they
        See not all clear.
    O for that night! where I in him
    Might live invisible and dim.

*Henry Vaughan*

# LADY GRIMOND

## THE GREATER CATS

THE greater cats with golden eyes
  Stare out between the bars.
Deserts are there, and different skies,
And night with different stars.
They prowl the aromatic hill,
And mate as fiercely as they kill,
  And hold the freedom of their will
  To roam, to live, to drink their fill;
  But this beyond their wit know I:
Man loves a little, and for long shall die.


  Their kind across the desert range
  Where tulips spring from stones,
  Not knowing they will suffer change
  Or vultures pick their bones.
  Their strength's eternal in their sight,
  They rule the terror of the night,
  They overtake the deer in flight,
  And in their arrogance they smite;
  But I am sage, if they are strong:
Man's love is transient as his death is long.

Yet oh what powers to deceive!
My wit is turned to faith,
And at this moment I believe
In love, and scout at death.
I came from nowhere, and shall be
Strong, steadfast, swift, eternally:
I am a lion, a stone, a tree,
And as the Polar star in me
Is fixed my constant heart on thee.
Ah, may I stay forever blind
With lions, tigers, leopards, and their kind.

*Victoria Sackville-West*

FROM:

THE RT. HON. LORD HAILSHAM OF ST. MARYLEBONE, C.H., F.R.S., D.C.L.

HOUSE OF LORDS,
SW1A 0PW

15th January, 1985

My dear Mary .

Thank you for your letter of 12th January 1985.

Alas, I have no favourite poem and those I like best are in
ancient tongues unsuitable for an anthology of this kind.  But in
translation (Prayer Book Version) I would place the 23rd Psalm.

At least there is no difficulty about copyright shd: you decide

to use it.

yrs :.

# LORD HAILSHAM

## THE TWENTY-THIRD PSALM

The lord is my shepherd: therefore can I lack nothing.

He shall feed me in a green pasture: and lead me forth
beside the waters of comfort.

He shall convert my soul: and bring me forth in the paths
of righteousness, for his Name's sake.

Yea, though I walk through the valley of the shadow of
death, I will fear no evil: for thou art with me, thy rod
and thy staff comfort me.

Thou shalt prepare a table before me: thou hast
anointed my head with oil, and my cup shall be full.

But thy loving-kindness and mercy shall follow me all the
days of my life: and I will dwell in the house of the Lord
for ever.

HOUSE OF COMMONS
# EDWARD HEATH

I love all beauteous things,
  I seek and adore them;
God hath no better praise,
And man in his hasty days
  Is honoured for them.


I too will something make
  And joy in the making;
Altho' to-morrow it seem
Like the empty words of a dream
  Remembered on waking.


*Robert Bridges*

# ELIZABETH JANE HOWARD

## REMEMBRANCE

THEY flee from me, that sometime did me seek
  With naked foot, stalking in my chamber.
I have seen them gentle, tame, and meek,
  That now are wild, and do not remember
  That sometime they put themselves in danger
    To take bread at my hand; and now they range
    Busily seeking with a continual change.


Thanked be fortune it hath been otherwise
  Twenty times better; but once, in special,
In thin array, after a pleasant guise,
  When her loose gown from her shoulders did fall,
  And she me caught in her arms long and small,
    Therewith all sweetly did me kiss
    And softly said, 'Dear heart, how like you this?'

It was no dream; I lay broad waking:
   But all is turned, thorough my gentleness,
Into a strange fashion of forsaking;
   And I have leave to go of her goodness,
   And she also to use newfangleness.
     But since that I so kindly am served,
     I would fain know what she hath deserved.

*Sir Thomas Wyatt*

# GLENDA JACKSON

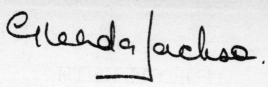

## NOT WAVING BUT DROWNING

NOBODY heard him, the dead man,
But still he lay moaning:
I was much further out than you thought
And not waving but drowning.

Poor chap, he always loved larking
And now he's dead
It must have been too cold for him his heart gave way,
They said.

Oh, no no no, it was too cold always
(Still the dead one lay moaning)
I was much too far out all my life
And not waving but drowning.

*Stevie Smith*

# PENELOPE KEITH

When your face came rising
Above my crumpled life
The only thing I understood at first
Was how meagre were all my posessions.
But your face cast a peculiar glow
On forests, seas and rivers,
Initiating into the colours of the world
Uninitiated me.
I'm so afraid, I'm so afraid.
The unexpected dawn might end,
Ending the discoveries, tears, and raptures,
But I refuse to fight this fear.
This fear—I understand—
Is love itself. I cherish this fear,
Not knowing how to cherish,
I, careless guardian of my love.
This fear has ringed me tightly.
These moments are so brief, I know,
And, for me, the colours will disappear
When your face has set. . . . .

*Yevgeny Yevtvshenko*
*1960*

# FELICITY KENDAL
# DAVID FROST

## TO HIS COY MISTRESS

Had we but World enough, and Time,
This coyness Lady were no crime.
We would sit down, and think which way
To walk, and pass our long Loves Day.
Thou by the *Indian Ganges* side
Should'st Rubies find: I by the Tide
Of *Humber* would complain. I would
Love you ten years before the Flood:
And you should, if you please, refuse
Till the Conversion of the *Jews*.
My vegetable Love should grow
Vaster than Empires, and more slow.
An hundred years should go to praise
Thine Eyes, and on thy Forehead Gaze.
Two hundred to adore each Breast:
But thirty thousand to the rest.
An Age at least to every part,
And the last Age should show your Heart.
For Lady you deserve this State;
Nor would I love at lower rate.
　But at my back I alwaies hear
Times winged Charriot hurrying near:
And yonder all before us lye

Deserts of vast Eternity.
Thy Beauty shall no more be found;
Nor, in thy marble Vault, shall sound
My ecchoing Song: then Worms shall try
That long preserv'd Virginity:
And your quaint Honour turn to dust;
And into ashes all my Lust.
The Grave's a fine and private place,
But none I think do there embrace.
  Now therefore, while the youthful hew
Sits on thy skin like morning dew,
And while thy willing Soul transpires
At every pore with instant Fires,
Now let us sport us while we may;
And now, like am'rous birds of prey,
Rather at once our Time devour,
Than languish in his slow-chapt pow'r.
Let us roll all our Strength, and all
Our sweetness, up into one Ball:
And tear our Pleasures with rough strife,
Thorough the Iron gates of Life.
Thus, though we cannot make our Sun
Stand still, yet we will make him run.

*Andrew Marvell*

# MONSIGNOR BRUCE KENT

## POEM FOR AN ADOPTED CHILD

Not flesh of my flesh
nor bone of my bone
but still, miraculous,
my own.
Never forget
for a single minute,
you didn't grow under my heart
but in it.

*Anon*

# FRANCIS KING
# MY LAST DUCHESS
## Ferrara

THAT'S my last Duchess painted on the wall,
Looking as if she were alive. I call
That piece a wonder, now: Frà Pandolf's hands
Worked busily a day, and there she stands.
Will't please you sit and look at her? I said
'Frà Pandolf' by design, for never read
Strangers like you that pictured countenance,
The depth and passion of its ernest glance,
But to myself they turned (since none puts by
The curtain I have drawn for you, but I)
And seemed as they would ask me, if they durst,
How such a glance came there; so, not the first
Are you to turn and ask thus. Sir, 'twas not
Her husband's presence only, called that spot
Of joy into the Duchess' cheek: perhaps
Frà Pandolf chanced to say 'Her mantle laps
'Over my lady's wrist too much,' or 'Paint
'Must never hope to reproduce the faint
'Half-flush that dies along her throat:' such stuff
Was courtesy, she thought, and cause enough
For calling up that spot of joy. She had
A heart—how shall I say?—too soon made glad,
Too easily impressed; she liked whate'er

She looked on, and her looks went everywhere.
Sir, 'twas all one! My favour at her breast,
The dropping of the daylight in the West,
The bough of cherries some officious fool
Broke in the orchard for her, the white mule
She rode with round the terrace—all and each
Would draw from her alike the approving speech,
Or blush, at least. She thanked men,—good! but thanked
Somehow—I know not how—as if she ranked
My gift of a nine-hundred-years-old name
With anybody's gift. Who'd stoop to blame
This sort of trifling? Even had you skill
In speech—(which I have not)—to make your will
Quite clear to such an one, and say, 'Just this
'Or that in you disgusts me; here you miss,
'Or there exceed the mark'—and if she let
Herself be lessoned so, nor plainly set
Her wits to yours, forsooth, and made excuse,
—E'en then would be some stooping; and I choose
Never to stoop. Oh sir, she smiled, no doubt,
Whene'er I passed her; but who passed without
Much the same smile? This grew; I gave commands;
Then all smiles stopped together. There she stands
As if alive. Will't please you rise? We'll meet

The company below, then. I repeat,
The Count your master's known munificence
Is ample warrant that no just pretence
Of mine for dowry will be disallowed;
Though his fair daughter's self, as I avowed
At starting, is my object. Nay, we'll go
Together down, sir. Notice Neptune, though,
Taming a sea-horse, thought a rarity,
Which Claus of Innsbruck cast in bronze for me!

*Robert Browning*

# BEN KINGSLEY

## SEA AND A RED ROSE

Following you
my soul was lost in a sea of people.
Exiled:
I carry my own dead body,
from which there is no response.
Time's root is moving fast.
The oath that was a closed lotus is slowly opening,
becoming a silent question.
In darkness, the vultures of memory are happy at their
feast to be.


They are trying to pluck out my eyes—
the eyes that were 'bottomless seas'.


Why did you leave me here alone—
exiled?
Sea and a red rose
and each mellow evening,
with some favourite poem,
I try to forget.
But they come back,

like flies in search of a wound,
and their noise fills me.
The chair that you have just left is still warm.
From the ashtray, blue smoke drifts upward.
Still I feel as if I were in a bed,
hiding my head for a lifetime.
You have taken back your love—
I wish I could give back
your memory.

*Nur Chowdhury*

## NEIL KINNOCK

# LAND OF MY MOTHERS

Land of my mothers, how shall my brothers praise you?
With timbrels or rattles or tins?
With fire.
How shall we praise you on the banks of the rhymneying
     waters,
On the smoky shores and the glittering shores of
     Glamorgan,
On wet mornings in the bare fields behind the Newport
     docks,
On fine evenings when lovers walk by Bedwellty Church,
When the cuckoo calls to miners coming home to
     Rhymney Bridge,
When the wild rose defies the Industrial Revolution
And when the dear old drunken lady sings of Jesus and a
     little shilling.


Come down, O girls of song, to the bank of the coal canal
At twilight, at twilight
When mongrels fight
And long rats bite
Under the shadows of pit-head light,
And dance, you daughters of Gwenllian,
Dance in the dust in the lust of delight.

And you who have prayed in golden pastures
And oiled the wheels of the Western Tradition
And trod where bards have danced to church,
Pay a penny for this fragment of a burning torch.
It will never go out.


It will gather unto itself all the fires
That blaze between the heavens above and the earth
      beneath
Until the flame shall frighten each mud-hearted hypocrite
And scatter the beetles fattened on the cream of
      corruption,
The beetles that riddle the ramparts of Man.


Pay a penny for my singing torch,
O my sisters, my brothers of the land of my mothers,
The land of our fathers, our troubles, our dreams,
The land of Llewellyn and Shoni bach Shinkin,
The land of the sermons that pebble the streams,
The land of the englyn and Crawshay's old engine,
The land that is sometimes as proud as she seems.

And sons of the mountains and sons of the valleys
O lift up your hearts, and then
Lift up your feet.

*Idris Davies*

# JAMES CALLAGHAN
# PHILIP LARKIN

# ELEGY WRITTEN IN A COUNTRY CHURCHYARD

The *Curfeu* tolls the Knell of parting Day,
The lowing Herd winds slowly o'er the Lea,
The Plow-man homeward plods his weary Way,
And leaves the World to Darkness, and to me.

Now fades the glimmering Landscape on the Sight,
And all the Air a solemn Stillness holds;
Save where the Beetle wheels his droning Flight,
And drowsy Tinklings lull the distant Folds.

Save that from yonder Ivy-mantled Tow'r
The mopeing Owl does to the Moon complain
Of such, as wand'ring near her sacred Bow'r,
Molest her ancient solitary Reign.

Beneath those rugged Elms, that Yew-Tree's Shade,
Where heaves the Turf in many a mould'ring Heap,
Each in his narrow Cell for ever laid,
The rude Forefathers of the Hamlet sleep.

The breezy Call of Incense-breathing Morn,
The Swallow twitt'ring from the Straw-built Shed,
The Cock's shrill Clarion, or the ecchoing Horn,
No more shall wake them from their lowly Bed.

For them no more the blazing Hearth shall burn,
Or busy Housewife ply her Evening Care:
No Children run to lisp their Sire's Return,
Or climb his Knees the envied Kiss to share.

Oft did the Harvest to their Sickle yield,
Their Furrow oft the stubborn Glebe has broke;
How jocund did they drive their Team afield!
How bow'd the Woods beneath their sturdy Stroke!

Let not Ambition mock their useful Toil,
Their homely Joys and Destiny obscure;
Nor Grandeur hear with a disdainful Smile,
The short and simple Annals of the Poor.


The Boast of Heraldry, the Pomp of Pow'r,
And all that Beauty, all that Wealth e'er gave,
Awaits alike th' inevitable Hour.
The Paths of Glory lead but to the Grave.


Forgive, ye Proud, th' involuntary Fault,
If Memory to these no Trophies raise,
Where thro' the long-drawn Isle and fretted Vault
The pealing Anthem swells the Note of Praise.


Can storied Urn or animated Bust
Back to its Mansion call the fleeting Breath?
Can Honour's Voice provoke the silent Dust,
Or Flatt'ry sooth the dull cold Ear of Death!

Perhaps in this neglected Spot is laid
Some Heart once pregnant with celestial Fire,
Hands that the Reins of Empire might have sway'd,
Or wak'd to Extacy the living Lyre.


But Knowledge to their Eyes her ample Page
Rich with the Spoils of Time did ne'er unroll;
Chill Penury repress'd their noble Rage,
And froze the genial Current of the Soul.


Full many a Gem of purest Ray serene,
The dark unfathom'd Caves of Ocean bear:
Full many a Flower is born to blush unseen,
And waste its Sweetness on the desert Air.


Some Village-*Hampden* that with dauntless Breast
The little Tyrant of his Fields withstood;
Some mute inglorious *Milton* here may rest,
Some *Cromwell* guiltless of his Country's Blood.

Th' Applause of list'ning Senates to command,
The Threats of Pain and Ruin to despise,
To scatter Plenty o'er a smiling Land,
And read their Hist'ry in a Nation's Eyes


Their Lot forbad: nor circumscrib'd alone
Their growing Virtues, but their Crimes confin'd;
Forbad to wade through Slaughter to a Throne,
And shut the Gates of Mercy on Mankind,


The struggling Pangs of conscious Truth to hide,
To quench the Blushes of ingenuous Shame,
Or heap the Shrine of Luxury and Pride
With Incense, kindled at the Muse's Flame.


The thoughtless World to Majesty may bow,
Exalt the brave, and idolize Success;
But more to Innocence, their Safety owe
Than Power and Genius e'er conspired to bless.

And thou, who mindful of the unhonour'd Dead
Dost in these Notes their artless Tale relate,
By Night and lonely Contemplation led
To linger in the gloomy Walks of Fate,

Hark how the sacred Calm that broods around
Bids ev'ry fierce tumultuous Passion cease
In still small Accents whisp'ring from the Ground
A grateful Earnest of eternal Peace

No more with Reason and thyself at Strife
Give anxious Cares and endless Wishes room
But thro the cool sequester'd Vale of Life
Pursue the silent Tenour of thy Doom.

*Thomas Gray*

# PRUE LEITH

## EXPOSED ON THE HEART'S MOUNTAINS

Exposed on the heart's mountains. Look, how small there!
look, the last hamlet of words, and, higher,
(but still how small!) yet one remaining
farmstead of feeling: d'you see it?
Exposed on the heart's mountains. Virgin rock
under the hands. Though even here
something blooms: from the dumb precipice
an unknowing plant blooms singing into the air.
But what of the knower? Ah, he began to know
and holds his peace, exposed on the heart's mountains.
While, with undivided mind,
many, maybe, many well-assured mountain beasts,
pass there and pause. And the mighty sheltered bird
circles the summits' pure refusal.—But, oh,
no longer sheltered, here on the heart's mountains . . .

*Rilke*

I have no favourite poem — or rather, I have many, and which one is at the top of the list at any moment depends on many things, particularly the mood I am in. But in any short list of my favourites there will always be the 130th sonnet of Shakespear, a dazzling exercise in sleight-of-hand, in which, after convincing the reader that the tone is entirely cynical, he reverses it in the final couplet, to make it one of the most beautiful and affecting love poems I know

Bernd Levin

# BERNARD LEVIN

## SONNET CXXX

My Mistres eyes are nothing like the Sunne,
Currall is farre more red, then her lips red,
If snow be white, why then her brests are dun:
If haires be wiers, black wiers grow on her head:
I have seene Roses damaskt, red and white,
But no such Roses see I in her cheekes,
And in some perfumes is there more delight,
Then in the breath that from my Mistres reekes.
I love to heare her speake, yet well I know,
That Musicke hath a farre more pleasing sound:
I graunt I never saw a goddesse goe,
My Mistres when shee walkes treads on the ground.
   And yet by heaven I thinke my love as rare,
   As any she beli'd with false compare.

*William Shakespeare*

# ARTHUR MARSHALL

## HENLEY REGATTA 1902

Underneath a light straw boater
In his pink Leander tie
Ev'ry ripple in the water caught the Captain in the eye.
O'er the plenitude of houseboats
Plop of punt-poles, creak of rowlocks,
Many a man of some distinction scanned the reach to
Temple Island
As a south wind fluttered by,
Till it shifted, westward drifting, strings of pennants
house-boat high,
Where unevenly the outline of the brick-warm town of
Henley
Dominated by her church tower and the sheds of
Brakspear's Brewery
Lay beneath a summer sky.
Plash of sculls! And pink of ices!
And the inn-yards full of ostlers, and the barrels running
dry,
And the baskets of geraniums
Swinging over river-gardens
Led us to the flowering heart of England's willow-cooled
July.

*John Betjeman*

# HRH PRINCESS MICHAEL OF KENT
# TIM RICE

## OZYMANDIAS

I met a traveller from an antique land
Who said: Two vast and trunkless legs of stone
Stand in the desert. Near them on the sand,
Half sunk, a shatter'd visage lies, whose frown
And wrinkled lip and sneer of cold command
Tell that its sculptor well those passions read
Which yet survive, stamp'd on these lifeless things,
The hand that mock'd them and the heart that fed;
And on the pedestal these words appear:
'My name is Ozymandias, king of kings:
Look on my works, ye Mighty, and despair!'
Nothing beside remains. Round the decay
Of that colossal wreck, boundless and bare,
The lone and level sands stretch far away.

*Percy Bysshe Shelley*

# JONATHAN MILLER

## THE PULLEY

WHEN God at first made man,
Having a glass of blessings standing by,
'Let us', said he, 'pour on him all we can:
Let the world's riches, which dispersèd lie,
                    Contract into a span.'


So strength first made a way;
Then beauty flowed, then wisdom, honour, pleasure;
When almost all was out, God made a stay,
Perceiving that, alone of all his treasure,
                    Rest in the bottom lay.


'For if I should',  said he,
'Bestow this jewel also on my creature,
He would adore my gifts instead of me,
And rest in Nature, not the God of Nature:
                    So both should losers be.

'Yet let him keep the rest,
But keep them with repining restlessness;
Let him be rich and weary, that at least,
If goodness lead him not, yet weariness
                    May toss him to my breast.'

*George Herbert*

# ROBERT MORLEY

## 'KNOW THYSELF'

Know then thyself, presume not God to scan;
The proper study of mankind is man.
Placed on this isthmus of a middle state,
A being darkly wise, and rudely great:
With too much knowledge for the sceptic side,
With too much weakness for the stoic's pride,
He hangs between; in doubt to act, or rest,
In doubt to deem himself a god, or beast;
In doubt his mind or body to prefer,
Born but to die, and reas'ning but to err;
Alike in ignorance, his reason such,
Whether he thinks too little, or too much:
Chaos of thought and passion, all confused;
Still by himself abused, or disabused;
Created half to rise, and half to fall;
Great lord of all things, yet a prey to all;
Sole judge of truth, in endless error hurled:
The glory, jest, and riddle of the world!

*Alexander Pope*

# THE SOLDIER

If I should die, think only this of me:
   That there's some corner of a foreign field
That is for ever England. There shall be
   In that rich earth a richer dust concealed;
A dust whom England bore, shaped, made aware,
   Gave, once, her flowers to love, her ways to roam,
A body of England's, breathing English air,
   Washed by the rivers, blest by suns of home.


And think, this heart, all evil shed away,
   A pulse in the eternal mind, no less
      Gives somewhere back the thoughts by England
      given;
Her sights and sounds; dreams happy as her day;
   And laughter, learnt of friends; and gentleness,
     In hearts at peace, under an English heaven.

*Rupert Brooke*

# NANETTE NEWMAN

## SONNET XVIII

Shall I compare thee to a summer's day?
Thou art more lovely and more temperate.
Rough winds do shake the darling buds of May,
And summer's lease hath all too short a date.
Sometime too hot the eye of heaven shines,
And often is his gold complexion dimmed;
And every fair from fair sometime declines,
By chance, or nature's changing course, untrimmed;
But thy eternal summer shall not fade,
Nor lose possession of that fair thou ow'st,
Nor shall Death brag thou wand'rest in his shade,
When in eternal lines to time thou grow'st.
    So long as men can breathe or eyes can see,
    So long lives this, and this gives life to thee.

*William Shakespeare*

COMMISSIONER OF POLICE
OF THE METROPOLIS

Sir Kenneth Newman QPM

NEW SCOTLAND YARD
BROADWAY LONDON SW1H 0BG

## SIR KENNETH NEWMAN

# STOPPING BY WOODS ON A SNOWY EVENING

Whose woods these are I think I know.
His house is in the village though;
He will not see me stopping here
To watch his woods fill up with snow.

My little horse must think it queer
To stop without a farmhouse near
Between the woods and frozen lake
The darkest evening of the year.

He gives his harness bells a shake
To ask if there is some mistake.
The only other sound's the sweep
Of easy wind and downy flake.

The woods are lovely, dark and deep.
But I have promises to keep,
And miles to go before I sleep.
And miles to go before I sleep.

*Robert Frost*

## FUTILITY

Move him into the sun—
Gently its touch awoke him once,
At home, whispering of fields unsown.
Always it woke him, even in France,
Until this morning and this snow.
If anything might rouse him now
The kind old sun will know.

Think how it wakes the seeds,—
Woke, once, the clays of a cold star.
Are limbs, so dear-achieved, are sides,
Full-nerved—still warm—too hard to stir?
Was it for this the clay grew tall?
—O what made fatuous sunbeams toil
To break earth's sleep at all?

*Wilfred Owen*

## LESTER PIGGOTT

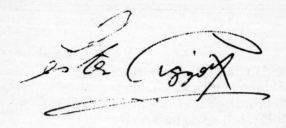

## JAYNE TORVILL &
## CHRISTOPHER DEAN

# THE OWL AND THE PUSSY CAT

The Owl and the Pussy-Cat went to sea
   In a beautiful pea-green boat.
They took some honey, and plenty of money
   Wrapped up in a five-pound note.
The Owl looked up to the stars above,
   And sang to a small guitar,
'O lovely Pussy! O Pussy, my love,
What a beautiful Pussy you are,
            You are,
            You are!
What a beautiful Pussy you are!'

Pussy said to the Owl, 'You elegant fowl!
  How charmingly sweet you sing!
O let us be married! too long we have tarried:
  But what shall we do for a ring?'
They sailed away, for a year and a day,
  To the land where the Bong-Tree grows,
And there in a wood a Piggy-wig stood,
With a ring at the end of his nose,
          His nose,
          His nose!
With a ring at the end of his nose.


'Dear Pig, are you willing to sell for one shilling
  Your ring?' Said the Piggy, 'I will.'
So they took it away, and were married next day
  By the Turkey who lives on the hill.
They dinèd on mince, and slices of quince,
  Which they ate with a runcible spoon;

And hand in hand, on the edge of the sand
   They danced by the light of the moon,
       The moon,
       The moon,
   They danced by the light of the moon.

*Edward Lear*

# ANDRÉ PREVIN

## THE TREES

The trees are coming into leaf
Like something almost being said;
The recent buds relax and spread,
Their greenness is a kind of grief.

Is it that they are born again
And we grow old? No, they die too.
Their yearly trick of looking new
Is written down in rings of grain.

Yet still the unresting castles thresh
In fullgrown thickness every May.
Last year is dead, they seem to say,
Begin afresh, afresh, afresh.

*Philip Larkin*

# CANDLES

The days of our future stand before us
like a row of lighted candles—
golden, warm and lively little candles.

The days gone by remain behind us,
a mournful line of burnt-out candles,
the nearest ones are still smoking,
cold candles, melted and bent.

I do not want to look at them—their form saddens me,
and it saddens me to recall their first light,
I look ahead at my lighted candles.

I do not want to look back, lest I see and shudder,
how quietly the sombre line lengthens,
how quickly the burnt-out candles multiply.

*C.P. Cavafy*

# EDUARDO PAOLOZZI

## EATING BAMBOO-SHOOTS

My new Province is a land of bamboo-groves:
Their shoots in spring fill the valleys and hills.
The mountain woodman cuts an armful of them
And brings them down to sell at the early market.
Things are cheap in proportion as·they are common;
For two farthings, I buy a whole bundle.
I put the shoots in a great earthen pot
And heat them up along with boiling rice.
The purple nodules broken,—like an old brocade;
The white skin opened,—like new pearls.
Now every day I eat them recklessly;
For a long time I have not touched meat.
All the time I was living at Lo-yang
They could not give me enough to suit my taste.
Now I can have as many shoots as I please;
For each breath of the south-wind makes a new bamboo!


A poem translated from the Chinese by Arthur Wakey

*From:* The Rt. Hon. J. ENOCH POWELL, M.B.E., M.P.

HOUSE OF COMMONS
LONDON SW1A OAA

## ENOCH POWELL

# TO THE NIGHTINGALE

O Nightingale, that on yon bloomy Spray
    Warbl'st at Eve, when all the Woods are still,
    Thou with fresh hope the Lovers heart dost fill,
    While the jolly hours lead on propitious *May*,
Thy liquid notes that close the eye of Day,
    First heard before the shallow Cuckoo's bill,
    Portend success in love; O if *Joves* will
Have linkt that amorous power to thy soft lay,
Now timely sing, ere the rude Bird of Hate
    Foretell my hopeless doom in som Grove ny:
    As thou from year to year hast sung too late
For my relief; yet hadst no reason why:
    Whether the Muse or Love call thee his mate,
    Both them I serve, and of their train am I.

*John Milton*

# ROBERT ROBINSON

## THE SUNLIGHT ON THE GARDEN

THE sunlight on the garden
Hardens and grows cold,
We cannot cage the minute
Within its nets of gold,
When all is told
We cannot beg for pardon.

Our freedom as free lances
Advances towards its end;
The earth compels, upon it
Sonnets and birds descend;
And soon, my friend,
We shall have no time for dances.

The sky was good for flying
Defying the church bells
And every evil iron
Siren and what it tells:
The earth compels,
We are dying, Egypt, dying

And not expecting pardon,
Hardened in heart anew,
But glad to have sat under
Thunder and rain with you,
And grateful too
For sunlight on the garden.

*Louis MacNeice*

# LORD SOPER

## SONNET IIV

Oh how much more doth beauty beauteous seem
By that sweet ornament which truth doth give;
The Rose looks fair, but fairer we it deem
For that sweet odour which doth in it live:
The Canker blooms have full as deep a dye
As the perfumed tincture of the Roses,
Hang on such thorns, and play as wantonly
When summer's breath their masked buds discloses:
But for their virtue only is their show
They live unwoo'd, and unrespected fade,
Die to themselves. Sweet Roses do not so,
Of their sweet deaths are sweetest odours made:
And so of you, beauteous and lovely youth,
When that shall vade, by verse distils your truth.

*William Shakespeare*

# BENJAMIN SPOCK

## TO THE NIGHT

SWIFTLY walk over the western wave,
   Spirit of Night!
Out of the misty eastern cave
Where, all the long and lone daylight,
Thou wovest dreams of joy and fear
Which make thee terrible and dear,—
   Swift be thy flight!


Wrap thy form in a mantle grey
   Star-inwrought!
Blind with thine hair the eyes of day,
Kiss her until she be wearied out,
Then wander o'er city, and sea, and land,
Touching all with thine opiate wand—
   Come, long-sought!


When I arose and saw the dawn,
   I sigh'd for thee;
When light rode high, and the dew was gone,
And noon lay heavy on flower and tree,

And the weary Day turn'd to his rest
Lingering like an unloved guest,
       I sigh'd for thee.


Thy brother Death came, and cried
       Wouldst thou me?
Thy sweet child Sleep, the filmy-eyed,
Murmur'd like a noontide bee
Shall I nestle near thy side?
Wouldst thou me?—And I replied
       No, not thee!


Death will come when thou art dead,
       Soon, too soon—
Sleep will come when thou art fled;
Of neither would I ask the boon
I ask of thee, belovéd Night—
Swift be thine approaching flight,
       Come soon, soon!

*Percy Bysshe Shelley*

## DAVID STEEL

# KILMENY

*An extract*

With distant music, soft and deep,
They lulled Kilmeny sound asleep;
And when she awakened, she lay her lane,
All happed with flowers in the greenwood wene.
When seven lang years had come and fled;
When grief was calm, and hope was dead;
When scarce was remembered Kilmeny's name,
Late, late in a gloamin Kilmeny came hame.
And O, her beauty was fair to see,
But still and steadfast was her ee!
Such beauty bard may never declare,
For there was no pride nor passion there;
And the soft desire of maiden's een
In that mild face could never be seen.
Her seymar was the lily flower,
And her cheek the moss-rose in the shower;
And her voice like the distant melodye,
That floats along the twilight sea.
But she loved to raike the lanely glen,
And keep afar frae the haunts of men;
Her holy hymns unheard to sing,
To suck the flowers and drink the spring.

But wherever her peaceful form appeared,
The wild beasts of the hill were cheered;
The wolf played blythely round the field,
The lordly byson lowed and kneeled,
The dun deer wooed with manner bland,
And cowered aneath her lily hand.
And when at eve the woodlands rung,
When hymns of other worlds she sung
In ecstasy of sweet devotion,
O, then the glen was all in motion!
The wild beasts of the forest came,
Broke from their boughts and faulds the tame,
And goved around, charmed and amazed;
Even the dull cattle crooned and gazed,
And murmured and looked with anxious pain
For something the mystery to explain.
The buzzard came with the throstle-cock;
The corby left her houf in the rock;
The blackbird alang wi' the eagle flew;
The hind came tripping o'er the dew;
The wolf and the kid their raike began,
And the tod, and the lamb, and the leveret ran;
The hawk and the hern attour them hung,

And the merl and the mavis forhooyed their young;
And all in a peaceful ring were hurled:—
It was like an eve in a sinless world!


When a month and a day had come and gane,
Kilmeny sought the greenwood wene;
There laid her down on the leaves sae green,
And Kilmeny on earth was never mair seen.
But O, the words that fell from her mouth,
Were words of wonder and words of truth!
But all the land were in fear and dread,
For they kendna whether she was living or dead.
It wasna her hame and she couldna remain;
She left this world of sorrow and pain,
And returned to the land of thought again.


*James Hogg*

# THE PANTHER
# JARDIN DES PLANTES, PARIS

His gaze, going past those bars, has got so misted
with tiredness, it can take in nothing more.
He feels as though a thousand bars existed,
and no more world beyond them than before.

Those supply powerful paddings, turning there
in tiniest of circles, well might be
the dance of forces round a centre where
some mighty will stands paralyticly.

Just now and then the pupils' noiseless shutter
is lifted.—Then an image will indart,
down through the limbs' intensive stillness flutter,
and end its being in the heart.

*Rainer Maria Rilke*

# DENIS THATCHER

This royal throne of kings, this sceptred isle,
This earth of majesty, this seat of Mars,
This other Eden, demi-Paradise;
This fortress built by Nature for herself
Against infection and the hand of war;
This happy breed of men, this little world;
This precious stone set in the silver sea,
Which serves it in the office of a wall,
Or as a moat defensive to a house,
Against the envy of less happier lands;
This blessed plot, this earth, this realm, this
    England,

*William Shakespeare*
*Richard II Act II Scene I*

# SUE TOWNSEND

## THE NIGHTINGALES NEST

Up this green woodland ride lets softly rove
& list the nightingale—she dwelleth here
Hush let the wood gate softly clap—for fear
The noise might drive her from her home of love
For here Ive heard her many a merry year
At morn & eve nay all the live long day
As though she lived on song—this very spot
Just where that old mans beard all wildly trails
Rude arbours oer the rode & stops the way
& where that child its blue bell flowers hath got
Laughing & creeping through the mossy rails
There have I hunted like a very boy
Creeping on hands & knees through matted thorns
To find her nest & see her feed her young
& vainly did I many hours employ
All seemed as hidden as a thought unborn
& where these crimping fern leaves ramp among
The hazels underboughs—Ive nestled down
& watched her while she sung—& her renown
Hath made me marvel that so famed a bird
Should have no better dress then russet brown
Her wings would tremble in her extacy
& feathers stand on end as'twere with joy

& mouth wide open to release her heart
Of its out sobbing songs—the happiest part
Of summers fame she shared—for so to me
Did happy fancies shapen her employ
But if I touched a bush or scarcely stirred
All in a moment stopt—I watched in vain
The timid bird had left the hazel bush
& at a distance hid to sing again
Lost in a wilderness of listening leaves
Rich extacy would pour its luscious strain
Till envy spurred the emulating thrush
To start less wild & scarce inferior songs
For cares with him for half the year remain
To damp the ardour of his speckled breast
While nightingales to summers life belongs
& naked trees & winters nipping wrongs
Are strangers to her music & her rest
Her joys are evergreen her world is wide
—Hark there she is as usual lets be hush
For in this black thorn clump if rightly guest
Her curious house is hidden—part aside
These hazel branches in a gentle way
& stoop right cautious neath the rustling boughs

For we will have another search to day
& hunt this fern strown thorn clump round & round
& where this seeded woodgrass idly bows
We'll wade right through it is a likely nook
In such like spots & often on the ground
Theyll build where rude boys never think to look
Aye as I live her secret nest is here
Upon this white thorn stulp—I've searched about
For hours in vain—there put that bramble bye
Nay trample on its branches & get near
—How subtle is the bird she started out
& raised a plaintive note of danger nigh
Ere we were past the brambles & now near
Her nest she sudden stops—as choaking fear
That might betray her home—so even now
We'll leave it as we found it—safety's guard
Of pathless solitudes shall keep it still
See there shes sitting on the old oak bough
Mute in her fears—our presence doth retard
Her joys & doubt turns every rapture chill
   Sing on sweet bird may no worse hap befall

Thy visions then the fear that now decieves
We will not plunder music of its dower
Nor turn this spot of happiness to thrall
For melody seems hid in every flower
That blossoms near thy home—these harebells all
Seems bowing with the beautiful in song
& gaping cuckoo with its spotted leaves
Seems blushing of the singing it has heard
How curious is the nest no other bird
Uses such loose materials or weaves
Their dwellings in such spots—dead oaken leaves
Are placed without & velvet moss within
& little scraps of grass—& scant & spare
Of what seems scarce materials down & hair
For from mans haunts she seemeth nought to win
Yet nature is the builder & contrives
Homes for her childrens comfort even here
Where solitudes deciples spend their lives
Unseen save when a wanderer passes near
That loves such pleasant places—Deep adown
The nest is made an hermits mossy cell

Snug lies her curious eggs in number five
Of deadened green or rather olive brown
& the old prickly thorn bush guards them well
& here we'll leave them still unknown to wrong
As the old woodlands legacy of song

*John Clare*

# PETER USTINOV

## HAIKU

Of the infinite steps to my heart
He scaled perhaps one
Or two . . .

# TED WILLIS

## THE TYGER

Tyger! Tyger! burning bright
In the forests of the night,
What immortal hand or eye
Could frame thy fearful symmetry?

In what distant deeps or skies
Burnt the fire of thine eyes?
On what wings dare he aspire?
What the hand dare seize the fire?

And what shoulder, and what art,
Could twist the sinews of thy heart?
And when thy heart began to beat,
What dread hand? and what dread feet?

What the hammer? what the chain?
In what furnace was thy brain?
What the anvil? what dread grasp
Dare its deadly terrors clasp?

When the stars threw down their spears,
And water'd heaven with their tears,
Did he smile his work to see?
Did he who made the Lamb make thee?

Tyger! Tyger! burning bright
In the forests of the night,
What immortal hand or eye,
Dare frame thy fearful symmetry?

*William Blake*
From *Songs of Experience*

# LORD WILSON OF RIEVAULX

## A PSALM OF LIFE
## WHAT THE HEART OF THE
## YOUNG MAN SAID TO THE
## PSALMIST

Tell me not, in mournful numbers,
  'Life is but an empty dream!'
For the soul is dead that slumbers,
  And things are not what they
    seem.

Life is real! Life is earnest!
  And the grave is not its goal;
'Dust thou art, to dust returnest,'
  Was not spoken of the soul.

Not enjoyment, and not sorrow,
  Is our destined end or way;
But to act, that each to-morrow
  Finds us farther than to-day.

Art is long, and Time is fleeting,
   And our hearts, though stout
      and brave,
Still, like muffled drums, are beating
   Funeral marches to the grave.


In the world's broad field of battle,
   In the bivouac of Life,
Be not like dumb, driven cattle!
   Be a hero in the strife!


Trust no Future, howe'er pleasant!
   Let the dead Past bury its dead!
Act,—act in the living Present!
   Heart within, and God o'erhead!


Lives of great men all remind us
   We can make our lives sublime,
And, departing, leave behind us
   Footprints on the sands of time;

Footprints, that perhaps another,
    Sailing o'er life's solemn main,
A forlorn and shipwrecked brother,
    Seeing, shall take heart again.

Let us, then, be up and doing,
    With a heart for any fate;
Still achieving, still pursuing,
    Learn to labour and to wait.

*H.W. Longfellow*

# MARY WILSON

*Mary Wilson.*

---

## PEACE

My soul, there is a country
　Far beyond the stars,
Where stands a wingèd sentry
　All skilful in the wars:
There, above noise and danger,
　Sweet Peace sits crown'd with smiles,
And One born in a manger
　Commands the beautous files.
He is thy gracious Friend,
　And—O my soul, awake!—
Did in pure love descend
　To die here for thy sake.
If thou canst get but thither,
　There grows the flower of Peace,
The Rose that cannot wither,
　Thy fortress, and thy ease.
Leave then thy foolish ranges;
　For none can thee secure
But One who never changes—
　Thy God, thy life, thy cure.

*Henry Vaughan*

# TERRY WOGAN

## THE SONG OF WANDERING AENGUS

I WENT out to the hazel wood,
  Because a fire was in my head,
And cut and peeled a hazel wand,
  And hooked a berry to a thread:
And when white moths were on the wing,
  And moth-like stars were flickering out,
I dropped the berry in a stream
  And caught a little silver trout.
When I had laid it on the floor
  I went to blow the fire a-flame,
But something rustled on the floor,
  And some one called me by my name:
It had become a glimmering girl
  With apple blossom in her hair
Who called me by my name and ran
  And faded through the brightening air.
Though I am old with wandering
  Through hollow lands and hilly lands,
I will find out where she has gone,
  And kiss her lips and take her hands;

And walk among long dappled grass,
   And pluck till time and times are done
The silver apples of the moon,
   The golden apples of the sun.

*W.B. Yeats*